CW00382421

WALKING
THROUGH THE
In the Birkenhead area
1940-1941
By NHC Tomlinson

Design & Origination
Ian Boumphrey - Desktop Publisher

Printed by
Design 2 Print
Llandudno
North Wales
LL30 1HH

Published by
Ian & Marilyn Boumphrey
"The Nook" 7 Acrefield Road
Prenton Wirral L42 8LD
Tel/Fax: 0151 608 7611
e-mail: ianb@wirralpc.u-net.com
http:/www.io-ltd.com/yw

ISBN 1-899241-07-8

CONTENTS

The author in Home Guard uniform, Silverdale Road, Oxton, 1941

INTRODUCTION

It is now over half a century since the 1940/1941 Blitz on Merseyside and those with first hand experience of those days are getting fewer in number. This fact prompted the notion of writing down this account of my own experiences of those times, first as a messenger in the ARP (Air Raid Precautions) and then as a member of the Home Guard. The intention was to provide my son, Martin, with a narrative which he may find interesting today and perhaps of greater historic interest when he is as old as I am now. Maybe others will be reminded of their own experiences of those times or be intrigued by the activities of at least some teenagers during the Blitz.

When war was declared on 3rd September 1939 I was aged 15 years 8 months and still at Park High school. I lived in Silverdale Road, Oxton, Birkenhead, on the corner of Wellington Road, with my mother, younger brother and sister. My father had died in 1937 and the business which he shared with his bachelor brother Henry Tomlinson had been carried on by the latter, who occupied part of the big house, with my mother employed as housekeeper.

My sister was evacuated to Maentwrog in Wales at the outbreak of war but, like me, my brother stayed at home. My Uncle Henry ('Harry') had been in the army in the First World War, and was very phlegmatic. There were to be a number of air raids before he deigned to take heed and leave his bed and get dressed. We had no shelter anyway and while my mother and brother sat in the living room or crouched in the hallway if things got hot, my uncle stood and watched from the door or chatted to a passing Air Raid Precautions (ARP) Warden. After many months of raids we had a Morrison shelter. [1]

---

1. A Morrison shelter was like a steel box with sides open but covered in heavy steel mesh. The inside could be made up with a bed and the top acted as a table. The strength was such that it would give protection against the house collapsing on top.

Chapter One
Preparing for War

During the crisis in 1938 trenches were dug around the rugby pitch by the sixth form boys at Park High School and the windows of the gym were sandbagged up to make it into an air raid shelter. The gym was about two thirds below ground level and was ideal for this purpose.

Then Chamberlain came back from Munich waving his piece of paper and saying that there would be peace in our time. The trenches were filled in and the sandbags taken down and everything returned to normal - but not quite. The country began seriously to prepare for war. During the next twelve months numerous Civil Defence pamphlets were issued:

Public Information Leaflet No. 1 "Some things you should know if war should come" - July 1939.
Leaflet No. 2 "Your gas mask - how to keep it and use it" and "Masking your windows" - July 1939.
Leaflet No. 3 "Evacuation why and how" - July 1939.
Leaflet No. 4 "Your food in war time" - July 1939.
Leaflet No. 5 "Fire precautions in war time" - July 1939.

These were followed by a further unnumbered leaflet titled *"Make your home safe now" - October 1939.*

It is interesting to note that Leaflet No. 3 on the subject of evacuation stated that *"although our defences are strong and getting stronger, some bombers would undoubtedly get through"*!

The Air Raids Precautions organisation was established in the remainder of 1938 and beginning of 1939 with the appointment of street wardens and ARP posts which took the form of a strengthened cellar in a private house whose owner was co-operative. The wardens had the job of canvassing all houses in their area and recording the number of occupants in each house.

ARP messengers were also enrolled from young boys over 15 and with a bicycle. I joined this force with great enthusiasm.

4

Just prior to the outbreak of war gas masks were issued to all the population through various depots which were established in great numbers so that no one had to travel far to get fitted. There was the basic civilian model in a cardboard container with a string carrying loop and a more robust ARP model, with seperate round glass eye pieces, which came with a strong canvas carrying bag. There was also a fitment to take a telephone insert for those manning telephones. The establishment of the ARP; the manufacture and issue of gas masks; the issue of advisory leaflets, as mentioned; and other preparations against air attacks was no doubt due to the foresight of many civil servants to whom a great deal is surely owed.

During the summer of 1939 the town decided to put on a show depicting an air raid to try and raise interest. In the North End of Birkenhead they were demolishing the notorious Dock Cottages. These were multi-storey council flats built in Victorian times and life in them must have been pretty grim. Demolition was down to about the second floor. An Air Raid Demonstration was advertised for late one afternoon and I and a number of my school friends eagerly made our way to the site after school.

The scheme was that a flight of Fairey Swordfish bombers would fly over and at the appropriate moment explosive charges, placed by the Royal Engineers in the remains of the buildings to represent bombs, would be detonated. Large crowds had turned up and were quite densely packed around the building. In due course the sound of aircraft was heard and the Swordfish came over in a shallow dive to the accompaniment of several loud bangs from the 'bombed' buildings. Unfortunately the charges threw up a large number of house bricks and these were seen rising into the air and tumbling towards the sightseers. There was a ripple throughout the crowd but there was little time to run and nowhere to run to. A number of people were hit by these flying bricks and in front of where I was standing a man in blue overalls was hit by a brick which ripped his pocket and scattered his loose change on the ground.

Ambulances were called and the first 'air raid casualties' were taken away. To us boys it was all very exciting and provided a talking point for days.

The purpose of the messengers in the ARP was to take information from the ARP post to HQ in Birkenhead in the event that communications via the telephone system were cut. Each post was supposed to have a messenger and two of my friends, Robert and Mike, joined as messengers and were at posts near to their homes. There was obviously quite a force of messengers and some individual in the Council who had economy in mind thought up the idea of getting the ARP messenger service to deliver the hundreds of letters which were addressed to the Wardens on the outbreak of war. These letters required the Wardens to attend their posts which were now allocated. A number of us spent many days and pedalled many miles delivering these letters and we came to know parts of the borough we had never seen before.

In the seven weeks of the summer holidays that year my school friends and I probably had only one worry and that was the problem of getting down to the "mountain" of homework which we had been given when school "broke up". Inevitably we left it with the intention of completing it in the last week before school went back. A few days before the end of the holidays, however, we were called back to school so the arrangements could be made for the evacuation of all those boys who had their names down for this scheme which had been laid down by the Government in all those areas considered vulnerable to air attack. All the keen boys were able to hand in their completed homework but I and a few others had nothing to hand over and could only explain that our intentions had been thwarted by the premature return to school. There was little the masters could say about our omission and they no doubt had too much on their minds to remonstrate very much. Some of us had avoided doing the work but it had taken the threat of war to make this possible.

Park High School was evacuated almost immediately to near Shotton Iron Works - a good target for bombers although it was never attacked! I and two of my close friends, Robert and Ken, were not evacuated and with some others found ourselves on holiday again but with a very obscure future.

On Sunday morning 3rd September it was announced by Chamberlain on the wireless that war had been declared. A few minutes after the address by the Prime Minister we went outside and watched all the barrage balloons ascending over Birkenhead. It was not long before the air raid warning went but nothing happened and it was soon followed by the all clear.

Chapter Two
The Phoney War

Although after the war ended we learned that the navy had been in action within an hour of the declaration of war and continued to fight the merciless war at sea, on land peace reigned and the forecasted devastating air raids did not take place until much later.

In the meantime sandbags made their appearance in many places as protection to important buildings, ARP posts, depots, etc., and all the Post Office letter boxes had their tops painted with a special green paint which changed colour if sprayed with a poison gas.

When the war began there was a 3.7 inch anti-aircraft battery at a site halfway down Holm Lane in Oxton (see picture below). Later this was replaced by more permanent 4.5 inch guns with other guns making their appearance in various parts of the borough. Not many, however, as they were one of the items of war of which the country was short. In Birkenhead Park air raid trenches were dug and a number of Lewis guns were set up to combat low flying aircraft. But if the balloon barrage worked there would be no low flying enemy aircraft! These Lewis guns were manned during the day and a few days after the war began a fleet of Hampden bombers flew up the Mersey; because of the level of jitters at the time and the lack of competence in aircraft recognition, the Lewis gunners opened up on them, resulting in one plane being hit. The town was building up a score of own goals . . .

3.7 inch guns in action (see this page).

The ARP had nothing to do so an exercise was held one evening. As a messenger I received my typed instructions which required me to ride a circular route along Shrewsbury Road up Tollemache Road, along Bidston Road and down Gerald Road back onto Shrewsbury Road again. I was to pedal this route at the beginning of the exercise, which was about 8pm, until the finish around 9pm. The idea was that as 'incidents' happened wardens could stop me or any other messenger as we went past and a message could then be taken to the ARP post where it could be telephoned to HQ. It was of course dark by then and I was able to use my specially adapted cycle lamp which was shaded by the insertion of white paper behind the glass from which was cut out a letter "M".

To me the exercise was anticipated with quiet excitement and I started off full of enthusiasm which was not initially dampened by it coming on to rain. I had a cape and the water ran off my helmet. The first circuit was made without seeing anyone connected with the ARP. The second circuit followed in the same way and on the third circuit I began to find the whole thing tedious. But then in Shrewsbury Road I saw a Corporation bus slewed across the road and ARP wardens milling around. This was it. I would now be given a message to take with all haste to our post in Kingsmead Road. But they just waved me past and all my interest evaporated. By this time anyway it was the end of the exercise and I rode home quite deflated.

The winter went by with no enemy activity over our part of the country and initial enthusiasms began to wane. In the Spring of 1940 we messengers were asked to go to a house in Prenton where we were given training in the use of a stirrup pump to extinguish an incendiary bomb. This was very helpful and was to stand me in good stead later on.

During the winter, although there were no raids to occupy the ARP, there was of course a total black-out at night. When there was no moon and heavy cloud the nights could be really black and going out meant feeling one's way carefully and avoiding things like lamp posts. There were many injuries and many deaths from road accidents as the lights on cars were reduced to a small slit which could easily go unnoticed by a pedestrian and gave little illumination to help the driver see where he was going. A lot of white paint was used along the kerbs and on steps to buildings to assist recognition in the dark.

The war, such as it was, seemed quite remote and although life had certain interesting and exciting aspects such as carrying a steel helmet marked with a letter "M" for messenger and having the special ARP gas mask different from those carried by ordinary civilians, plus of course the occasional air raid training exercise, I do not think my friends and I really believed German bombers would ever appear overhead. Such an event still seemed most unlikely. It couldn't happen where we lived. Somewhere else perhaps.

Then on 10th May 1940 the Germans started their offensive in Europe and in six weeks it was all over with most of the British army evacuated via Dunkirk. Perhaps now the war in the air over England would hot up after all.

Our home, at 'lucky' 13, Silverdale Road, Oxton, is seen on the right, on the corner of Wellington Road, next to the Post Office.

Chapter Three
The Blitz Begins - June 1940

It was in June, on the 25th, between 1 o'clock and 2 o'clock in the morning, that I was awakened by the sirens, the nearest being mounted on the top of St Saviour's Church tower which was only a few hundred yards away and the sound was deafening. I immediately got out of bed and dressed as quickly as possible with great excitement and anticipation. Getting on my bicycle I rode along Bidston Road towards Kingsmead Road where my post was situated. After the warning sirens had died down there was an ominous silence and as I rode along there was no one to be seen. There was a prickly sensation at the back of my neck and the feeling of being alone with everyone else having taken cover. I felt very responsible and proud of being "on duty". My route took me past the entrance to Chetwynd House which was occupied by an army unit and as I came abreast of the gates I was somewhat surprised to be challenged by a sentry with the usual *"Who goes there?"*. I replied firmly *"OK, messenger reporting to post"* and I was allowed to pass.

After arriving at the post I was asked to look for some of the wardens who were supposed to be on their beat but I could not find them. Shortly afterwards I was given a cup of tea and then the All Clear sounded and we all dispersed for home. On my way back I was challenged again and I had to produce my Identity Card. An hour had elapsed since the warning but there had been no gun fire or any other sound of action.

No further warnings sounded until 15th July when the sirens sounded in the daytime at 1.15pm. I was at home at the time and rushed to the post in two minutes flat. This time I saw a German plane flying quite high going south over Oxton followed by shell bursts which seemed frustratingly near but not unfortunately on target. There were also bursts of machine gun fire but the plane was too high up for this to be effective. The post during the day was manned mainly by women. This first tiny taste of action was exhilarating and I was able to collect my first pieces of anti-aircraft shell splinters.

Collecting shell splinters became a popular hobby with many schoolboys particularly the nose caps of the big "ack ack" shells and the smaller shiny aluminium nose caps of the Bofors shells. Eventually there was so much of it that interest waned.

A few days later on 21st July at 1.35am in the morning the sirens sounded again. There were lots of searchlights over New Brighton way and the sound of gunfire. Opinion was that a plane or planes were engaged in dropping magnetic mines in the mouth of the Mersey. When the all clear went half an hour later I cycled to the bottom of Kingsmead Road where I had agreed to meet Robert and Mike at the end of any raid. The intention was to discuss our experiences. They were not there however, much to my disappointment.

It was only a couple of nights later on 23rd July that I was awakened at 2am by the sound of heavy gunfire and I stood at the window watching the searchlights and the gunflashes. Then all went quiet and I went back to bed but then I could again hear the sound of a German plane, with its peculiar throbbing engine note. Suddenly the sirens sounded and as I was dressing there was again heavy gunfire. I reached my post in seven minutes by which time the action had died down. After about half an hour the All Clear went and I went to our meeting place and met Robert and Mike. While we were having a chat we saw a searchlight and a few minutes later we could hear a German plane again which seemed to be coming from the west. The next thing there was a series of brilliant flashes and heavy explosions followed by gunfire. We immediately set off again for our posts but by the time I reached my post it had gone quiet again so after a cup of tea I set off for home. On the way I met Robert and he and I stood and chatted to the sentry at Chetwynd for a while. It was 3.30am before I got to bed.

It was 2nd August before the sirens sounded again at 11.30pm. In fact the first I heard was the sound of a German plane and when I got out of bed I could see searchlights. The sirens then sounded and after quickly dressing I was off to my post, being somewhat delayed by trouble with the three-speed gear on my bike. On the way two special constables stopped me and told me to completely switch off my already heavily shaded cycle lamp. They must have had the jitters to make this request as the glow was extremely feeble and some light was permitted and indeed was necessary. In the hour to the All Clear there was no action. The sound of enemy planes and action from the ground pre-empting the siren warning was to become a feature of numerous raids in the future. Two days later on the 4th August at six minutes past midnight the siren

11

awakened me, and again on my way to the post I was told to extinguish my cycle lamp. By 2am I was back in bed.

The sirens sounded at just gone 11pm on the 7th August with no action, and then on the 8th August at 12.33am the warning went, but just before it did a stick of about six bombs was dropped across Prenton. For the first time we were made aware of the heart-stopping sound which a bomb makes, and the apprehension of approaching danger as a stick of bombs bursts in a line which always seems to involve you at some point - at least in your imagination.

Some damage was done and one person was killed. A story at the time (in fact true) was that in one house that was hit, which was the home of the owner of Bunneys in Liverpool, the maid was killed and she was German-born. Being true this made it very ironic that the first casualty in the area was German.

A few searchlights were seen and after the All Clear at nearly 2am a plane was heard diving over Oxton very low, and about half an hour later gunfire was heard over Wallasey.

Of course the next day I joined the crowds who went to see the damage. The war had really arrived in my home town.

About the same time the next night planes were heard over New Brighton and searchlights were active. Next there were flashes and whistling sounds of bombs were heard followed by explosions. The warning sirens then followed. During the period up to the All Clear at 1.10am there was the sound of distant explosions and flashes could be seen but there was no local activity.

10th August. Six died and four injured in Wallasey. Mine-laying occurred on many nights in August.

On the night of 12th August, I awoke some time after 11pm to the sound of planes overhead and the sky full of searchlights. I immediately got dressed. It was then that the sirens went followed shortly afterwards by distant flashes in the sky and the sound of about three bombs dropping. No other action followed until after the All Clear at midnight when a plane was heard overhead again and I returned to my post for about ten minutes.

Many alarms followed in August on the nights of 13th, 14th, 15th, 18th and 19th, and on several occasions the alarm sounded twice during the night. On 17th/18th August bombs hit docks in Liverpool damaging the LMS Goods Depot and part of the overhead railway. On 19th August the first alarm was at 11pm when heavy explosions were heard towards Thingwall and Heswall, but these were probably anti-aircraft guns. After arriving home a plane was heard overhead and was fired at by the AA batteries, but firing ceased when green and red Very lights were seen, so presumably it was British. The All Clear had gone at 11.52pm, but at 2.14am the sirens sounded again, but only after I had been awakened first by the sound of explosions. On rushing to the window I was met by the amazing sight of a sky lit up by searchlights and streams of brilliant tracer shells and shell-bursts. The 4.5 inch battery in Holm Lane was firing for the first time and the sound was shattering, shaking the house with each salvo. The plane could be clearly seen in the searchlights over Liverpool surrounded by shell-bursts from small guns firing red tracer and brilliant white tracer from the heavier guns. These latter were referred to as "flaming onions". At one point there was a prolonged burst of machine gun fire, probably from a ship in the river. Then machine gun tracer fire from the plane could be seen aimed at a barrage balloon which was sent down in flames. This action took place prior to the sounding of the warning siren and in fact there was no action between the warning and the All Clear at 2.57am.

After one night's activities some wardens thought they heard bombs coming down in the area covered by my ARP post in Kingsmead Road but no explosions had been heard. This indicated the possibility of unexploded bombs or time bombs in the area and the next morning everyone was allocated part of a road to check on.

I was responsible for a section of Shrewsbury Road and it necessitated calling on each house and requesting permission to search the garden back and front for unexploded bombs which would be evident by a hole surrounded by disturbed earth. I can still remember the look of alarm on the faces of people who answered the door and to whom I explained my purpose in calling. Despite their apparent alarm however there was no panic and I was left to search around the grounds of each house. Nobody volunteered to accompany me however.

I did not find any bombs in my area but of course I was late arriving at school, which had started again as so many had returned from evacuation to rejoin those who had remained at home. It so happened that that morning the headmaster, James Ure, decided to clamp down on latecomers, air raids or no air raids. All those who were not at school on time were paraded to see the headmaster in his study and to give an explanation for their crime of being in late. When it came to my turn to go in his study he glared at me and said *"Well, why are you late?"* I replied, *"I have been looking for unexploded bombs, sir."* Poor Jimmy Ure, who hated the idea that the war should have any effect on his school, had no option but to dismiss me. He didn't say a word but just waved his hand for me to go. I cannot believe that any other school boy in history has given such a reason for being late at school.

The intensity of the raids had slowly built up since the beginning of June and even at the end of August they were only of short duration and little action. This gradual introduction meant that everyone had the chance of getting used to the noise and danger and routines were established which became automatic by the time the big raids started. As small as these raids were they were experienced on Merseyside before London received any bombing.

In the last four nights of August a total of 455 tons of HE bombs and 1029 incendiary canisters were dropped. The bending by the British of the radio direction beams, which the Germans were using to find their target, meant that a lot of this load was dropped elsewhere than on Liverpool docks.

About the end of August a meeting of all the ARP workers and other Defence Personnel in the area was held one evening in Birkenhead School. I cannot remember the reason for this meeting but it was of relatively short duration and came to an end while it was still daylight. There was quite a large crowd at the meeting and most streamed out of the back of the school across the quadrangle towards the playing fields. I suppose we were almost across the quadrangle when there was the roar of three German bombers at quite low altitude tearing across the fields towards the town. In an instant everyone was diving for the ground in a panic and I remember seeing someone's steel helmet run past me on its rim like a wheel. The mass of people below must have been clearly seen by the bomber crew but amazingly they did not open fire with their machine guns. What the planes did do was to zoom up towards the height of the balloon barrage and whilst two of the planes carried on across the town the third plane flew between two lines of balloons. As it came abreast of a balloon there was a short burst of machine gun fire and within a minute there were three balloons going down in flames. One could imagine the panic of the balloon crews as they winched in at high speed a flaming mass of balloon, which might engulf the winch itself together with the operator, whilst trying to avoid about a mile of steel cable falling across the town damaging buildings and blocking roads. The sirens eventually sounded and everyone made their way to their posts but there was little action following.

31st August: Wallasey Town Hall was damaged and the Customs House set ablaze. A bomb burst alongside the battleship, *The Prince of Wales*, fitting out in Cammell Laird, Birkenhead. This ruptured the hull and the ship listed dangerously. Birkenhead fire brigade took two and a half days to pump her out.

The intensity of raids built up over the next few months and the nightly strafe became part of life. Not every night, but there would be periods when the frequency of raids was high and then there would be calm for several nights.

The last few weeks at school while awaiting the results of the School Certificate Exams was spent, in company with several other lads, pasting brown paper strips on the interior of all the school windows. The idea of the paper strips was to cut down the amount of flying glass fragments caused by bomb blast. I do not think this was very effective in practice because the force of the blast was usually so great as to shatter windows into hundreds of flying pieces and the paper strips were just ripped to shreds. We had an hilarious time doing the job and a great deal of paste was used on the windows and elsewhere.

Attacks of comparatively minor intensity took place in September, October and most of November - about a raid every other night. On 5th and 6th September a big fire engulfed the Liverpool Grease, Oil and Chemical Company in Norfolk Street and much of the stained glass in the cathedral was blown in. On 18th/ 19th September a bomb hit a wing of Walton Prison, killing a number of prisoners. Two nights later Central Station, Liverpool, was hit and there were major fires in warehouses and timber yards in Bootle. On 24th and 25th September more warehouses were hit.

Chapter Four
The Raids Intensify - September 1940

On the morning of 14th September a Junkers 88 photographed Sealand, Liverpool and Birkenhead and that night a railway shed and sidings at West Alexandra Dock at Bootle were hit and mines were dropped in Liverpool Bay. On the night of 15th September nine Heinkels bombed Liverpool and Birkenhead with widespread damage. Of course for many of the raids relatively few aircraft took part, but on other occasions there would be dozens of planes arriving over a period of hours.

On 26th and 27th September there was a big attack and widespread damage in Liverpool, and in Birkenhead the Argyle Theatre was gutted. In the LMS/GWR marshalling yard in Birkenhead a train-load of HE bombs was hit by incendiaries but was saved by three railway workers who were decorated for their bravery. By the end of September 327 Merseysiders had been killed and 590 seriously injured.

In one of these raids a bomb landed in the park near my school. It did not go off and therefore the whole school was evacuated and fitted into the Girls' School at the other side of the park for the several days that it took the engineers to dig down to the bomb and defuse it. What a time was had by all the lads mixing with the girls, particularly as we always goggled at their short maroon skirts with the split up each side. Unfortunately for me I had already left to take up my first job in the office of the Gas Company in Hind Street, Birkenhead.

As September progressed so did the intensity of the raids and the defences became more noisy and spectacular. The sky would be lit up by streams of tracer from Bofors guns which besides shooting at aircraft flying at low altitude would also have a go at shooting out the flares which were dropped and which turned night into brightest day. The bigger guns being manned on the ships in dock and anchored in the river joined in, many firing the brilliant white tracer shells.

Of course the opening of most raids was announced by the searchlights probing the sky for a target. First one finger of light then others until dozens of beams criss-crossed the sky and so throughout the raid. It was fascinating to see on

16

occasion the bright gleam of a plane caught in a beam onto which would lock more beams and then of course the guns would follow. But I never saw a hit and the target would twist away and be lost. Searchlights, coloured tracer, reverberating explosions and perpetual gun fire with frequent whistles from falling bombs followed by the rising and falling glow of reddish light from bomb bursts produced a scene more spectacular than any fireworks display in peacetime could ever hope to achieve.

As aircraft approached from over Wales one heard the gun battery in Holm Lane firing outwards from the town, the sound in the main being the clank of the breeches opening and shutting. Then as the planes came overhead and the guns had swivelled round to point over the town the concussion felt at home in Silverdale Road was colossal. The back door threatened to come in at each salvo and the whole house shook. Each raid consisted of several hours of a rising cacophony of sound followed by a quietening off as planes left the area to be followed by the next group.

Slatey Road Police Station damaged 29 September 1940 and later demolished.

The weather played a part in the timing and frequency of raids and good weather with a good moon was a likely time for a raid. People referred to a 'bomber's moon' and waited in anticipation of the sounding of the sirens. Social life was naturally affected and governed to a large extent by the air raids. During periods when raids were frequent people stayed at home and near a shelter but a few nights without raids and people soon started visiting each other again. The cinemas kept going and if a raid came in the middle of a performance a warning was projected onto the screen indicating that a raid was imminent. Usually the film was continued after those who wished to leave had left. But then it could be a matter of 'out of the frying pan into the fire' for those that left. Probably most public local shelters would be full. Public transport could be seriously reduced, if running at all, and there were the ever present falling shell splinters with which one had to contend. Without a steel helmet one felt a little naked particularly when these splinters could be heard whirring down and the sparks when they struck the road surface could be seen.

On the 3rd October a German bomber strafed Speke airport in daylight. That month 136 were killed and 167 injured on Merseyside.

The basement shelter of the school in Durning Road, Liverpool, was hit on 28th and 29th November with 180 people killed and 96 injured.

Parachute mines were dropped, some of which failed to explode. One unexploded mine penetrated a gas holder in Garston and it had to be defused after the gas and water was pumped out.

After some three weeks respite there were raids on 20th, 21st and 22nd December. More mines. Exchange Station was hit and 42 people were killed who were sheltering under a viaduct arch. The raid on the 21st lasted from 6.48pm to 8.40pm and from midnight to 5.15am. Seventy-four people in a shelter in Anfield were killed. St. John's fish market was burned down and as it was stocked with poultry for Christmas it gave off a very appetising smell.

In Wallasey most residents in a women's home were killed and survivors were asphyxiated beneath rubble by ruptured gas mains.

On 24th December, Christmas Eve, there was an air raid but it was thankfully small and ineffective. There were raids on 27th, 29th and 31st December. Over 40 ships were sunk or damaged in raids on the river and docks.

As 1940 came to an end the air raids had become part of life. In Birkenhead the bombing was very widespread, not concentrated on the docks as it was obviously intended to be. There was bomb damage in various parts of the town and the sight of ruined houses, piles of bricks, fluttering curtains at glassless windows and the grey white powder of brick and mortar dust in many streets was quite common.

Chapter Five
A Typical Big Raid

Although one came to expect the raids, particularly if the weather was right with a 'bombers moon', when the first note of the warning sounded it nevertheless came as a shock or at least a surprise. As mentioned previously there was a siren on the tower of St Saviour's Church, which was close by Silverdale Road, and the noise was deafening. By the time the warning had died down people had cleared the streets if it was daylight and except for the ARP wardens, or anyone else with duties, everyone had gone to their shelter. A most ominous silence then reigned as if everyone was holding their breath. If the raid had come during the hours of darkness the first noise to break the silence was the sound of de-synchronised aero engines. The throb-throb of the first German bombers. This noise would get louder and then there would be a series of bright flashes followed almost immediately by the crash of the anti-aircraft guns. With the 4.5 inch battery half way down Holm Lane the flash and the noise in Silverdale Road was intense. The throbbing overhead became louder and the first finger of a searchlight probed the sky to be followed by numerous others trying to latch onto the bomber which would soon be joined by more.

In many raids the next event was the dropping of parachute flares by the enemy to illuminate the target. These flares came down very slowly and the light was so intense that if one walked in the middle of the road one felt that every bomber crew could see you. To counter the flares the Bofors guns began firing their strings of tracer shells at them and it was quite fascinating to watch the marksmanship. Only a few flares were actually extinguished this way. The gun barrage now became thunderous from all sides of the town and the almost musical note of falling bombs would be heard. If the bombs were close the sound was like an express train approaching at a frightening speed to be followed by earth-quaking explosions.

Shortly after the opening phase the sky in various places over the town would glow red as fires took hold and the sound of fire engines would be heard and other vehicles racing round the town to bomb "incidents". The gun barrage rose in intensity and then fell away as one wave of raiders passed over and then would start up again as further planes were detected coming in from North Wales across Wirral. This pattern would be repeated hour after hour sometimes up to four and five o'clock in the morning. The ships in the river contributed to the defensive barrage many firing heavy guns with the brilliant white and red tracer shells. As the barrage moved overhead there would be showers of lethal shell splinters falling like rain and striking sparks on the road surface. Sometimes a whirring sound as a particularly big piece such as a nose cap could be heard. The raid could have comparative lulls but the night overall consisted of one long crashing noise, whistles of falling bombs and brilliant light, and in areas where bombs had fallen there would be a covering of grey dust over everything from pulverised plaster and mortar and bricks. Frequently during the raid the electric light would falter or go off altogether for a time. In some streets gas mains would be ignited and the next day in some areas gas pressure would be low for cooking. Water also could fall in pressure as water mains were fractured and to counteract this many parts of the town had emergency water tanks erected which could be used for fighting fires.

When the All Clear finally went it was a case of getting to bed for an hour or two of sleep before setting off to work with the expectation that the next twenty-four hours would be a repeat of the previous.

Chapter Six
Joining the Home Guard - 1941

1941 arrived but in January and February bad weather kept down the raids and there was none of real intensity. In this period 55 people were killed and 48 injured.

In the new year two things happened to me. First I changed jobs from working for the Gas Corporation at their offices in Hind·Street near Central Station to a job in the office of Unilever Export Limited at Lever Bros, Port Sunlight. Secondly I decided that being a messenger in the ARP was not exciting enough. The telephones had always worked and I had never had to dash to HQ with an urgent message. Being young the wardens were very protective and whilst there was any air activity I was not allowed out of the shelter. This did not suit me at all. I wanted to be out and about and see what was going on. I was now 17 so I resigned from the ARP and joined the Home Guard. My old school friend Robert followed suit.

Whilst in the Home Guard we had to stand guard at Beresford Road HQ on certain nights and there were also pickets to be manned. There was an anti-parachutist picket on Wirral Ladies Golf Course and a fire picket at Harrowby Road drill hall. Such duties were spaced out and therefore during most of the raids we were off-duty so Robert and I used to meet after the sirens had sounded and we would go off walking around the town during the raid looking for excitement. When the sirens sounded we would get dressed usually in our Home Guard uniform with respirator and steel helmet and walk towards each other to meet somewhere in Shrewsbury Road. He was coming from Tollemache Road in Claughton so we met somewhere between Beresford Road and Howbeck Road. Many nights were of course pitch dark with no moon and mainly cloud cover so it was necessary to attract attention to our presence and recognise one another by whistling some bars of *Poet and Peasant*. There were occasions when we would find ourselves perhaps a hundred yards apart both taking cover by lying flat in the gutter while a stick of bombs fell nearby - that experience was quite frightening. If one was anywhere on the line of a falling stick of bombs the noise was like being near an express train, every few seconds being punctuated by a loud explosion, each explosion getting nearer until, hopeful they were over you and receding.

The question in one's mind at the time was whether one of the sticks was going to land on your patch.

1941 was the year when the raids increased in ferocity and also when they came to an end at least as far as Merseyside was concerned.

As I have already explained both Robert and I were now in the Home Guard. In many of the raids we were able to walk around and because they sometimes lasted several hours I suppose we covered many miles. In our wanderings we came across 'incidents' which had just happened. One evening we arrived at Woodchurch Road School where a surface shelter full of people had been hit. A number of people were killed and some were injured. Another night in Village Road Oxton a house was hit but by the time we arrived had been reduced to a heap of bricks with a lone figure digging among the rubble. When we met him he just said *"my father is under this lot somewhere"*. We eventually left with ARP salvage teams digging away.

At the time both Robert and I were very keen on Strauss music and when the film *The Great Waltz* came to the Savoy in Birkenhead we went along to see the film. The cinemas were not exactly full at the time for obvious reasons, but this particular evening it was not a bad attendance; that is until there was an announcement on the screen of an air raid warning. We were determined to see the film and remained seated with a small handful of other people whilst outside we could hear a lot of gun fire and many heavy detonations. When we came out at the end of the film there was quite a merry raid in progress with no public transport running so we slowly walked the three miles back home to the accompaniment of much noise and shell fire.

With the increase in the weight of the raids the defences were strengthened. There were more mobile guns and rocket batteries established in various places. These batteries consisted of 24 or 48 projectors and one of these was set up in a field near Beryl Road, Noctorum. One particular evening I was on guard duty at the Home Guard HQ on the corner of Wellington Road and Beresford Road. A lively raid was in progress. A group of us was standing outside the front gate chatting when we heard a German plane chugging overhead away from the town. Suddenly there was an extremely loud roar and a spectacular display of fire in the sky as the battery of rockets near Beryl Road let fly. The rockets soared together to their set altitude and exploded in a rolling crash followed by relative silence. Surely such a weapon could shoot down the German plane - but he was still there droning into the distance, to our great chagrin.

As part of the increased defences, smoke screens were laid by a special army force. Along predetermined routes in the town according to the wind direction long convoys were parked consisting of special lorries in the back of which was a stove-like contraption fed by a tank of fuel oil pumped in by a small petrol engine. The oil was burned in the stove with insufficient air resulting in thick black clouds of smoke being emitted from the chimney. There were dozens of these vehicles in a convoy manned by army personnel who wore uniforms absolutely filthy with oil and soot.

The city designated as always receiving these raids was of course Liverpool but it should be understood that a raid on Liverpool was also a raid on Birkenhead and Wallasey. In fact a large part of Wirral came in for a lot of the bombs which were aimed at the shipping in the Mersey and the docks on both sides of the river. The approach to the river and the docks was of course over Wirral and the increasing weight of the gun barrages meant that a lot of the aircraft dropped bombs short.

Officers of No 3 Company 4th Cheshire (Birkenhead) Battalion Home Guard at "Chetwynd", Oxton.

23

Chapter Seven
The Bombing Comes Closer to Home - March 1941

12th March 1941 was my mother's birthday and I do not suppose she ever forgot it. From information gathered since that day it is known that a big attack was launched at Liverpool with a total of 339 bombers and the main weight of the attack actually fell on Birkenhead and Wallasey. The bombers came from France, Holland, Belgium and Norway. The moon was full - a good 'bomber's moon'. British Fighter Command put up a total of 178 night fighters to counter this attack and had planes patrolling the enemy airfields in France from which bombers were taking off. Very few enemy aircraft were shot down.

If I was not on duty I usually walked along to Rose Mount in Oxton Village to talk to either Marjorie (later to become my wife) or her sister Kay, and we would stand in the doorway of their newspaper shop. I think that on this particular night I was talking to Kay when the sirens went. The searchlights lit up the sky and it was not long before the guns were in action and planes were overhead. Soon a good raid was in progress and there were many bombs coming down over the town. At one point there was a roaring sound of a descending bomb close by and we ducked into the shop although what protection that would have given I do not know. I was in fact late enough to see the explosion about a 100 yards up Rose Mount by the wall of a front garden. It is most likely that this was an ack-ack shell which had not exploded at the intended height. Because of the length of many raids the guns were getting worn barrels, and as the rifling of the barrel twists the shell in flight and releases the safety device which prevents any possibility of it bursting within the barrel, the reduced twist caused by worn rifling was resulting in quite a few shells failing to burst. They inevitably burst when they hit the ground, however. After each gun barrage it was becoming common to hear one or two falling shells. There were a number around Oxton and one which had hit a house on the corner of Gerald and Shrewsbury Road did so much damage that the house was eventually pulled down. Nearby in Alton Road some soldiers billeted in one of the houses were standing outside when a shell burst among them and they were blown to bits.

Sometime later there was a succession of fiery glows in the sky at various points over the town followed by very loud detonations, and one was not far

24

Above: Part of the remains of the 'Caernarvon Castle', Oxton, after the air raid of 12/13 March 1941. St Saviour's Church is in the background.

Below: Numbers 17 to 23 Euston Grove damaged the same night (see page 27).

25

away over Oxton. At the time I did not appreciate the significance of these particular effects but we were fascinated by the fact that the big plate glass window of the shop had been sucked out about six inches at the bottom but was otherwise still unbroken and in place at the top. It finally slid out and smashed.

I eventually decided to make my way home as the raid was continuing at a good pace and it appeared that it would be a long night. As I walked up Willan Street a German bomber came overhead flying low with the rear gunner firing a stream of tracer towards the Holm Lane gun battery. When I approached the end of Wellington Road about a quarter of a mile from home I was aware that the road was covered in fragments of brick and other debris which built up the nearer I got to Silverdale Road. When I arrived home at Silverdale Road an incredible sight greeted me. Whilst number 13 where I lived still stood the rest of the road on the same side up to Bidston Road consisting of several Ruabon brick terraced houses and a couple of big semi-detached houses at the top of the road had gone. All that was left of the terraced houses was the front wall which leaned out at about 30 degrees. Gone was the Caernarvon Hotel, the smithy at the rear of the pub, Heaton and Tabb the interior decorators and the house that was behind. The roof of Saint Saviour's church was virtually removed and in Wellington Road the big three-storey Victorian semis were badly damaged. In fact I later walked with my Uncle Harry through huge holes in the dividing walls from one house to the next checking to make sure that no one was injured. On the other side of Silverdale Road houses were severely damaged and the whole area looked absolutely devastated. There was no one in 13 Silverdale and I eventually located my mother and my younger brother in a cellar shelter further down Silverdale Road. This was a house belonging to a Miss Robinson and her brother and although all of them knew that there had been a near miss they had no conception of the havoc that had been caused in the road. It was only about six o'clock in the morning when my mother and brother came back up the road that they were aware of the damage.

My Uncle Harry had in fact been in the Caernarvon Castle that evening having a drink when about nine o'clock a bomb had landed in the field across the road only about 75 yards away. The result of this bomb was that everyone decided to go home and there was a rush to get away.

It was not long after this that a mine dropped just behind the pub and caused all the damage. One person in the Caernarvon was killed but incredibly no other person was injured. Even the vicar escaped in an amazing way; when I met him he was somewhat dazed and was wearing a helmet with a huge dent in it. Apparently he had been in the road when the mine dropped and a brick had hit him on the head but he had been saved by his helmet. In the First World War he had been wounded in the head but he had been saved from fatal injury by his helmet!

The house, although still standing, was in a mess. Most windows were broken although some miraculously survived. One window in the upstairs lounge had been sucked out of the wall complete in its frame without breaking and this we managed to push back into place and nail firm. Many tiles were off the roof and ceilings and walls had lost plaster. The blast had gone straight through the kitchen and the larder which was divided from the next room by a laths and plaster wall. Only the laths were left and all the crockery in the kitchen was smashed to smithereens, also a cut crystal decanter which my mother had stored in the larder. We had to borrow cups to have a drink of tea. Subsequently various kind neighbours gave us cups, plates and other crockery. That day, 13th March, I stayed at home helping to clear up and make the house habitable. In the morning we had a visitor from some council department who condemned the house as unfit to live in but my uncle was adamant that we remain and so we did. On the night of 13th March I stayed at the house of my friend Robert and when a raid started we all went down into their cellar shelter. I didn't like it down there a bit and eventually said I would go up to my room to bed which I did. For a while I lay there listening to the raid and imagining I could hear the flapping of a parachute mine but as I was very tired I eventually fell asleep. The next night I was back home again but sleeping in a downstairs room as my room at the top of the house was in such a mess.

My friend Mike's house at 25 Euston Grove was so badly damaged the same night that his mother and father, although unharmed, had to crawl out of the cellar through the coal hole (*see picture on page 25*).

During the day of 13th March a squad of soldiers was brought in to clear up some of the debris particularly the remains of the Caernarvon Hotel. A lot of crates of beer were salvaged and the troops were given a good ration.

St Saviour's Church had a lot of damage to the tower and the roof was severely damaged and had to be covered with tarpaulins. That roof was still under repair when I was married in September 1948 and we have photographs of the wedding showing a lot of scaffolding.

On 14th March I was back at the office at Port Sunlight and found that everyone had spent 13th March clearing up there. A large bomb had landed about 150 yards away destroying MacFisheries Bakery near the bowling green. The blast from this bomb had caused a lot of damage to the office roof and smashed a great deal of glass. Many years later that roof leaked every time it rained.

The raid on the night of 12th March fell mainly on Birkenhead and Wallasey. An estimated 270 groups of incendiary bombs fell on the built up area starting more than 500 fires of which 9 reached major proportions. A total of over 300 high explosive bombs and 60 parachute mines exploded. The mines devastated whole blocks of houses. Machinery and dockside handling equipment was destroyed. Two ships and the 200 ton lift *Mammoth* were sunk and a further three ships suffered damage. Three flour mills were damaged, the Vacuum Oil Company's installation at Birkenhead was practically destroyed and both gas holders at Wallasey were burnt out. In this attack and the smaller raid the following night 631 people were killed and a similar number injured.[2] One German bomber, a Junkers 88, was brought down in the Mersey estuary. All the crew parachuted to safety. The pilot, a Feldwebel Guenther Unger, came down in shallow water off Wallasey and took over an hour to wade ashore through the many deep channels before giving himself up to the Home Guard.

2. In Landican cemetery there are six unmarked graves in CE section 9 references 375-380 inclusive. In these graves lie the remains of 24 unidentified victims of the Blitz, no doubt from the night of 12 March. The graves also include the remains of Mildred Holyoake, Rose O'Calaghan, Catherine O'Calaghan, W McMullen, Elsie McIntosh and Catherine Edge. There are no headstones or other markings on the graves except the serial numbers. Whilst the country has ensured that all the remains of military personnel are buried with a headstone the town has not seen fit to erect headstones for these civilian victims of the war! The references are:

375 - 1 unidentified buried   12/4/41   376 - 1 unidentified buried   23/4/41
377 - 1   "   "   26/4/41   378 - 4   "   "   31/3/41
379 - Mildred Holyoake, Rose O'Calaghan + 3 unidentified   buried   21/3/41
380 - Catherine O'Calaghan, W McMullen, Elsie McIntosh and Catherine Edge +
            14 unidentified buried 21/3/41

Because of the severe damage to the houses round about many people were having to leave the district. One family, before leaving, very kindly handed us a bucket full of eggs preserved in isinglass. This was a much appreciated gift and we had a supply of eggs which lasted us many weeks.

One of the more curious aspects of war is the effect of rumour. On arriving home one day from the office my mother informed me that a German bomber had come down not far away at Mere Farm which was part of Noctorum on the outskirts of the town. I immediately cycled off towards the spot and on the way met crowds of other people coming from all directions to see the crash site. Some asked me where it was and I could only indicate that I had been told it was at Mere Farm. We never found the crashed bomber. There never was one. How did the rumour start and so many people become aware of it?

In April there were three raids and it was during one of these that I was still in bed when I heard a peculiar metallic pattering sound in the road outside. Then I was aware of bright white light shining through cracks in the blackout over the window. I realised immediately that a canister of incendiaries had dropped and quickly got dressed and rushed out. Some bombs were burning in the road but were being attended to by ARP wardens. Along the road however one of the remaining large Victorian semi-detached houses had a bomb burning on the roof. Wardens were already in the house so I entered and went up the stairs. On the first landing I came across one warden standing there with a bucket of water and stirrup pump. He was looking at the ceiling and said he would wait for the bomb to burn through from the roof. It struck me that by this time the whole house would be in flames so I went on up into the attic, where I looked for a boarded up hole in one of the walls which I knew was an entry into the eaves of the roof. I found this entry and more wardens appeared agreeing that I should climb through to find the bomb. I pulled the hose with me and crawled under the eaves to where I could see flame and hear the sizzling of the bomb, shouting in correct fashion *"water on"*. This was the signal for a warden to start pumping, and using the fine spray nozzle I saturated the flames and the bomb, eventually putting it out. I then shouted *"knock off make up"* as I had been taught and the wardens stopped pumping and that was the end of that.

The next day however one of the owners of the house called at 13 Silverdale and asked my mother to thank me for saving their house and handed over an envelope addressed to me. Inside was five shillings as a reward. Of course this was quite unexpected and five shillings was quite a significant sum in those days. Still, five shillings for saving a very large three storey house!

A few days later my brother and I were in the shed in the back yard with one of the unburned incendiary bombs in the vice. The German incendiary bomb which was dropped in clusters was beautifully made but if it dropped in soft earth it could be smothered and after the initial ignition it would go out. Such was the bomb we had in the vice and we were sawing a piece off it with a hacksaw to put on the kitchen fire and watch the magnesium burn with a very white flame. Whilst we were sawing away the chief fire warden for the area walked into the yard to speak to my uncle. He had a most alarmed expression on his face when he saw what we were doing and left very promptly.

It was around this time that the enemy started fixing an explosive charge to the tail of some incendiaries to discourage people from extinguishing them.

As has already been explained the objective of the enemy was the port of Liverpool but a very large area received a lot of bombs. The route of the enemy aircraft was over North Wales and from the direction of Anglesey and with the build up of the ack-ack defences around Liverpool particularly over Wirral, many planes tended to bomb early on seeing the barrage being put up by the guns. People across Wirral had to take cover for the whole of the time of each raid as many rural areas received quite a lot of bombs. Some people must have felt relatively safe however if they were out in the country, and those people living in the house beside the market gardens situated in the fields between Noctorum and Woodchurch must have felt they had little to fear. This was a well built house comprising two dwellings semi-detached.

On a Saturday following one of the raids my section of the Home Guard were taking part in an exercise which took us down the fields past this particular house. When we arrived at the house we found that it had been hit by a bomb which had gone through the roof and had blown out all the walls so that the whole structure had collapsed with the roof roughly intact on the heap of bricks. All the inhabitants had been killed and ARP squads were at work digging them out. When we arrived one woman was being pulled out from a tunnel made in the debris and alongside the hedge were several bodies covered in sheets. What an incredible chance had killed these people: that bomb could have fallen anywhere within two or three square miles and it would have fallen harmlessly in a field.

One of the defences against the bombers was called by the codename STARFISH. This took the form of lights and fires which were sited in an isolated position and which were lit when the bombers approached their target, the intention being that they would mistake the fires for the main target and drop their load of bombs. Such a site was located on the Middle Eye of Hilbre Island in the Dee estuary and this stratagem diverted quite a lot of bombs from the main target area, particularly during the raids at the beginning of May.

Robert 'ready for action' in Home Guard uniform,
Silverdale Road, Oxton, 1941.

Chapter Eight
The "May Blitz" 1941

On the night of 1st May there was a light raid lasting from about 11pm to 1 o'clock in the morning, in which a total of 48 tons of HE bombs and 4,000 incendiaries were dropped. The next night a raid lasted from 10.45pm to 2.45am and there then followed on 3rd May the worst raid of all for Liverpool with 363 tons of HE bombs and 49,700 incendiaries. Several hundred fires were started in Liverpool alone and many more on Wirral. One of the more spectacular events was the explosion of the munitions ship Malakand in Huskisson Dock, Liverpool.

Fire brigades from many other parts of the country were brought in, from Scunthorpe, York, Wakefield, West Hartlepool, Derby, Doncaster, Huddersfield and Leicester. Had the wind been stronger a fire storm could have resulted. Robert and I at the height of the raid stood in Fairview Road at the top of Bennetts Hill in Oxton and watched an unbroken line of fire over Liverpool stretching from as far left as one could see to as far right. This was the most incredible background for the many searchlights and slowly rising strings of tracer shells and rolling clouds of smoke. The continuous sound of the gun barrage and the chug-chug of German aircraft added the last touches to a scene which almost defies description. No matter how spectacular fireworks displays have been since the war they have never ever begun to compare with this raid and many others which took place during this period of the war.

The smell of burning was in the air for several days and the fires in the docks were burning several days later when my company of the Home Guard were driven past on the way to the rifle ranges at Altcar.

Further raids took place on 4th, 5th, 6th and 7th May and each night there was a huge exodus from Liverpool to the outlying countryside but the majority returned during the day.

On this side of the water there were many bombs and much damage. To avoid total loss of the buses it had become the practice at Laird Street Bus Depot to disperse them each night around Birkenhead Park (the steering wheel of each bus was removed as it was still necessary to ensure that any parked vehicle was made immobile in the event of invasion). Despite this however many buses were destroyed or damaged and I found myself riding to the office at Port Sunlight on buses without any windows or without a roof. It was still a bit chilly in the morning with the wind whipping around one's hands and feet.

By the end of the seven nights people were, if nothing else, very tired as each night there was little time left after the All Clear for more than an hour or two of sleep. At the office one still had to book in at 8.30 hours and an explanation was required if one failed to be in by this time.

Soon after this week of raids a friend of mine who also worked at Port Sunlight was on a few days holiday. Rich lived in Noctorum and had come across a party of Royal Engineers working down in the fields on an unexploded bomb. This bomb had been there several days and was obviously being treated as one which had failed to explode as opposed to a delayed action bomb. Because it was being treated as unexploded and was in an isolated situation the engineers knocked off work at the end of the day, as opposed to working around the clock as was the case in a residential area. Rich suggested that we go down and look at the bomb in the evening which we did.

The engineers had dug down about thirty foot in steps and there at the bottom of the hole was a large bomb of about half a ton. We were quite fascinated and climbed down to inspect it more closely. The fins were all twisted as it had ploughed into the ground and on the side of the bomb was a round cavity which had obviously contained the detonator. This was reassuring and after giving the missile a good examination we climbed out of the hole and looked down at the monster. Then, because we could not resist the temptation, we both picked up a small stone and threw it down the hole at the bomb to hear a satisfying 'clonk' as they hit. We then picked up some bigger stones and gave the bomb a good pelting: after all, the bomb had been defused.

A couple of days later I met Rich again and he said *"You know that bomb? Well I went down the next day to watch the engineers get it out. You know what?"*, he said, *"They rolled it over and took out another fuse!"*. So although it had not exploded it was still alive - and we had been throwing stones at it! Rich had taken some of the explosive from this bomb and gave a piece to me.

The 4th Battalion No 3 Company Home Guard fighting patrol, pictured at "Chetwynd", Oxton, with their winning cup after a competition against other Home Guard Companies in April 1942 (see opposite page).

However, when lit with a match it burned harmlessly with a smokey flame.

May saw two further raids, one on the 29th and the other on the 31st, with more damage in various parts but mainly in Gladstone and Alexandra Docks, Liverpool. There were further small raids on the 25th June, 24th July and the 1st November and on the 10th January 1942 the last bombs fell on Merseyside, during which raid 15 people were killed when a row of houses in Upper Stanhope Street, Liverpool were hit.

And so after eighteen months the blitz on Merseyside came to an end. Outside London, Liverpool was the most bombed city in the country because of its strategic importance as the main supply port. Birkenhead had shared this bombing and indeed Wirral from West Kirby across to Birkenhead and the River Mersey had received bombs, the number of which increased the nearer the area was to the Mersey.

On the basis of the total number of houses, in 1939, of the four boroughs - Liverpool, Bootle, Wallasey and Birkenhead, Bootle suffered most having the greatest percentage killed and injured with almost all the houses either destroyed or damaged. However, Birkenhead came next in terms of casualties and over 78% of houses either destroyed or damaged.

The Home Guard was still 'on guard' of course although the threat of invasion had largely disappeared. Training had become more sophisticated and there were inter-company competitions (see photograph on page 34).

The Blitz was a unique and incredible experience and to me as a young man of 17 years a most exciting time. With my friend Robert I had walked for hours in the raids and had also spent a number of duties in the Home Guard on picket in various places such as on Wirral Ladies Golf Links with the shrapnel raining down and pattering in the grass. We had walked around many areas from the centre of town to Claughton, Prenton and Oxton. We had taken cover as bombs fell or the rain of shrapnel became too concentrated and we had visited the aftermath of many incidents. The people we met during our walks were of course ARP personnel otherwise the streets were empty, everyone else having taken cover in shelters of one sort or another, including that most favourite shelter 'under the stairs'. It was an amazing period of history which will never again be repeated, because bombardment from the air is now more sophisticated with great accuracy which can confine damage mostly to the military target at which it is aimed. Also the time taken over the target is very short; not the hours that were endured during the Blitz. It was also a time when everyone was a comrade. People were helpful and friendly under fire and all classes of society were involved and affected. This is something which vanished after the war and will never happen again. Without doubt it was a most wonderful experience to have lived through the Blitz although I feel sure my mother, being of an older generation, took a different view.

In January 1942 I volunteered for the Royal Armoured Corps and was called up on 29th April joining the 58th Training Regiment at Bovington, Dorset. After six months training I joined the 108th RAC Regiment - Lancashire Fusiliers at Rufford Abbey, Nottinghamshire, which had Churchill Tanks and later Shermans. Late in 1943, having attended the Highland Fieldcraft Training Regiment at Kingussie, Inverness-shire (the forerunner of the Outward Bound

Schools after the war), I passed the War Office Selection Board for a commission and went to Sandhurst in 1944. I was commissioned in July 1944 and after spending some time at Catterick Depot eventually sailed for India just before Christmas. My posting was to the Indian Armoured Corps at Jhansi but eventually I was transferred back to the British Army spending some time at the depot in Poona and then joining the 146th Duke of Wellington Regiment. However, the war in Europe and the Far East ended whilst we were still re-equipping.

I served four years eight months in the army all of which was spent perpetually training and never getting near the action. Except for a few days spent in London during the period of the V1 flying bombs, which I watched coming over with fascination, I never experienced in the whole of my army career the excitement or fear that the blitz had provided at the end of my school days.

~ ~ ~ ~ ~ ~ ~

ACKNOWLEDGEMENTS

I would like to thank the following people who either loaned me their photographs or provided information used in this book:-
Ian Boumphrey; Violet (nee Tomlinson) Davies; Ernest Dugard, Tony Fowles, John Lindsey, David Lock; Colin Millington and Mike Pagan.

Also Brian Dunn and Albert Nute for their help and the many other people, too many to list, who offered information.

Lastly, but not least, my thanks to my son, Martin, and Ruth who gave much encouragement and did the initial typesetting.